Unsung gifts – *the Spirit* *at work in the New Testament*

NICK FAWCETT

kevin
mayhew

First published in 2002 by
KEVIN MAYHEW LTD
Buxhall, Stowmarket, Suffolk IP14 3BW
Email: info@kevinmayhewltd.com

9 8 7 6 5 4 3 2 1 0

ISBN 1 84003 919 1
Catalogue No 1500511

Cover design by Angela Selfe
Edited by Katherine Laidler
Typesetting by Louise Selfe
Printed and bound in Great Britain

Contents

To Cora Gore
in grateful memory of Ernie.
With heartfelt thanks for all the kindness
you both showed in so many ways

Acknowledgements

The publishers wish to express their gratitude to the following for permission to include copyright material in this book:

Church House Publishing, Great Smith Street, London, SW1P 3NZ, for the prayer from *Series 3: Morning and Evening Prayer,* © The Central Board of Finance of the Church of England; the Archbishops' Council, 1999.

Carmelite Monastery, Quidenham, Norwich, Norfolk, NR16 2PH, for the prayer 'In me, my God, be present'.

Cambridge University Press, The Edinburgh Building, Shaftesbury Road, Cambridge, CB2 2RU, for the two extracts from The Book of Common Prayer (adapted), the rights in which are vested in the Crown.

Bible quotations are taken from the New Revised Standard Version of the Bible, copyright © 1989 by the Division of Christian Education of the National Council of the Churches of Christ in the USA. Used by permission. All rights reserved.

Introduction

'Now there are various gifts, but the same Spirit; various ministries, but the same Lord; different types of service, but the same God working through all of them' (1 Corinthians 12:4-6). We have probably all heard those words on more than one occasion, and we would all probably applaud the sentiment they express, yet how seriously do we take them? All too often, debates about the Holy Spirit become bogged down in controversy concerning speaking in tongues, prophecy or works of healing; in other words, centred around arguments concerning so-called charismatic renewal. Personally, I think it very sad that gifts of the Spirit are identified in such a narrow way, and that some Christians are afraid of talk of the Spirit while others appear to claim a monopoly of spiritual gifts. The irony is that Paul only refers to tongues because of the trouble they were causing in Corinth, and all the gifts he mentions are placed firmly below the three great gifts of faith, hope and love. In reality, there is, and can be, no exhaustive list of spiritual gifts. They can cover virtually anything, from talking to listening, praying to encouraging, caring to sharing.

To illustrate that point, this study course focuses upon six individuals whose life and witness made a significant contribution to the early Church. The gifts they exhibited were not those we would automatically describe as spiritual, nor were they necessarily the only gifts they had, but each played a part in furthering the cause of Christ. First, there was Ananias, with his willingness to say yes. Next, comes Barnabas, someone who was always ready to encourage. Next, there is James, whose open-mindedness and willingness to listen is a gift we need to nurture as much today as ever. Then there is Epaphras, a man who was 'always wrestling with prayer'. Then Epaphroditus, whose enthusiasm in the cause of Christ nearly cost him his life. Finally, we turn to Luke, whose gift of 'being there' was perhaps the most simple yet special of all.

I apologise in advance that these individuals are all men. This reflects the cultural bias of the New Testament rather than my own, and it is one that I have attempted to counterbalance through another book in this study series, *Women of Faith – what they teach us*. There is nothing innately 'male' in the gifts represented here; indeed, some may feel there is nothing particularly spiritual either, but I would contend otherwise. When we talk of the Holy Spirit in terms of a few rarefied and unusual gifts, we run the risk of divorcing faith from daily life, rooting it instead in some kind of esoteric experience. For me, the strength of the early Church lay in the fact that faith touched every part of people's experience, and that as often as not it was the ordinary that was transformed by the Spirit's touch.

Too many people have grown suspicious of talk of the Holy Spirit due to the emphasis placed on certain gifts. Too many others have found themselves worrying that they have not received the Spirit, because such gifts are not evident in their life. It is my hope that this booklet will show that the Spirit moves in numerous ways and in all kinds of people. We put limits on that at our peril.

Nick Fawcett

Leader's notes

I suggest using the material in this book as follows:

- Each session begins with a traditional prayer, followed by a short paragraph introducing the overall theme. It is worth reading this aloud, to set the scene for the session.

- After this I have included 'Activity' sessions, designed to break the ice and to encourage informal reflection on the theme of the study. Allow ten minutes or so for these, but do not allow them to dominate the session. Remember that some of the Activity sessions need props, so don't forget to prepare carefully beforehand.

- Next comes a Bible passage (my own paraphrase unless otherwise stated). This should be read aloud and then time given for group members to ponder its meaning quietly.

- Ideally, group members need to have read the 'Comment' section before the meeting, in which case you will need to have circulated booklets in advance of the first session. Alternatively, extend the period of quiet after the reading so that participants can read this section at their own pace.

- The 'Summary' section highlights the key points of the Comment. The leader should read this aloud before inviting people's thoughts on the subject so far.

- Allow discussion to develop and introduce as appropriate the questions provided in the Discussion section. It may be appropriate at this point to bring in the passage suggested for further reading, though you may prefer to leave this, as I have done, to round off the theme nearer the end.

- Pause for prayer, using the prayer provided, a prayer of your own, or a time of quiet/open prayer.

- After allowing ample time for discussion, read the meditation to draw people's thoughts together. The meditations in weeks 1 and 2 are taken from my first book *No Ordinary Man*. Other meditations were written specially for this book.

- Briefly, outline the suggestions for action. Invite any further ideas from among the group. From the second week onwards, you might also give people the opportunity to share how they applied the suggestions from the previous week.
- Finally, end the meeting in prayer, using either the prayer provided or your own.

Prayer

Holy Spirit,
  we rejoice that,
  as you came to the Apostles on that day of Pentecost,
  so you keep on coming to us today;
  making yourself known in different ways,
  at different times and in different places,
  but always there,
  constantly moving in our lives.
We rejoice that you come to us in times of need –
  bringing comfort in times of sorrow,
  courage in times of fear,
  peace in times of trouble,
  and hope in times of despair.
We rejoice that you come when we forget our need of you –
  challenging,
  searching,
  refining,
  cleansing;
  inspiring us to greater vision and renewed commitment.
We rejoice that you come to us in power –
  releasing unimagined potential,
  imparting unexpected gifts,
  cultivating undreamed-of fruits.
Holy Spirit,
  come to us now,
  opening our minds to your guidance,
  our hearts to your love,
  and our lives to your purpose.
Breathe upon us,
  fill and enthuse us,
  and send us out in the service of Christ,
  in his name.
Amen.

First week

Ananias: Ready to say yes

Opening prayer

Guide us, Lord,
  in all our doings with your gracious favour,
  and further us with your continual help;
  that in all our works begun,
  continued,
  and ended in you,
  we may glorify your holy name,
  and by your mercy attain everlasting life;
  through Jesus Christ our Lord.
Amen.

Series 3: Morning and Evening Prayer

Introduction

Ask someone to lend you fifty pounds and what will you get? Almost certainly, very little, unless it happens to be your lucky day. Offer to _give_ someone fifty pounds and it will be a very different story; indeed, you may well find yourself fending off eager volunteers only too willing to benefit from your unexpected largesse! Whether we say yes or no depends very much on what the question may be, on what is expected of us and what is offered in return. Most of the time, the question foremost in our minds is 'What's in it for me?' Very rarely is our first consideration 'What can I do for you?' So when Ananias became conscious that God was calling him to visit the house where Saul was staying in Damascus, he was understandably less than enthusiastic at the prospect. He knew very well what to expect from that encounter, or at least he thought he did: arrest, imprisonment and almost certain death. It's not the most enticing of job specifications, is it? Yet God, it turned out, had other ideas. Saul, apparently, had changed, having met with Jesus on the Damascus Road and realised the error of his ways. From then on he would be the servant rather than opponent of Christ. How would you have felt at that reassurance? Would you have accepted it straightaway, shrugging off any lingering doubts with a casual 'OK, that's all right then'? I wouldn't. I think I'd have needed a lot more convincing and persuading before I was ready even to consider changing my no to a yes. Ananias was different. He heard, he listened, he responded, and through his faith the way was opened for Paul to find acceptance in the Church and to embark on his astonishing work of mission. When God calls, our natural inclination may often be to say no, for it may look hard, if not downright impossible. That, though, is to see things from *our* perspective rather than his. If he wants us to do something, he is able to help us accomplish it, provided, that is, we do one thing – provided we first say yes.

Activity

Yes or no? (see page 68).

Reading: Acts 9:10-19a

There was a certain disciple in Damascus by the name of Ananias, and the Lord spoke to him in a vision, saying, 'Ananias.' He answered, 'I'm here, Lord.' The Lord said to him, 'Get up and go to the street known as The Straight, and there look in the house of Judas for a man called Saul of Tarsus. He is praying at this very moment, and in a vision he has seen a man called Ananias enter and lay hands on him so that he might recover his sight.' But Ananias protested, 'Lord, I have heard from many people about this man, about all his cruelty to your saints in Jerusalem, and how he has come here now with authority from the chief priests to arrest all those who confess your name.' However, the Lord told him, 'Go, for he is my chosen vessel through which I will make my name known before Gentiles and kings, and before the children of Israel; I personally will reveal to him everything he must suffer for my name's sake.' So Ananias left and entered the house. Then, laying on his hands, he said to Saul, 'Brother Saul, the Lord has sent me – Jesus who appeared to you on your way here – in order that you may see again and be filled with the Holy Spirit.' And immediately what seemed to be scales fell from Saul's eyes, and he could see once more. Then he rose and was baptised, and after eating some food, he felt strengthened.

Comment

Of all the passages in the New Testament, few are better known or more often preached on than Acts chapter 9, but the strange thing is that all the attention tends to be given to the wrong person. It's understandable, for that one was to become central to the growth of the Christian Church, his story and writings making up a significant part of the New Testament, while the other was to disappear without trace; yet, for me, this chapter belongs fair and square to Ananias. It is he rather than Saul who is the real hero of the hour, the contribution he makes to the work of Christ out of all proportion to the fleeting moments he spends on the New Testament stage. In him, we glimpse someone of extraordinary courage and faith; a man who, in a variety of ways, was willing to say yes to God, and whose example offers abiding lessons for today.

Yet, before we move on to those, it is heartening, given our own repeated lack of faith, to remember that Ananias' initial reaction was to say no. When he heard that Saul was heading for Damascus, it seems that he decided to do precisely what most of us would have done in his shoes; namely lie low and keep quiet. He knew as well as anyone the reputation of this man, and was well aware that he had come to Damascus with one aim in mind: to destroy the church there as he had done so ruthlessly elsewhere. When Paul was in town it spelt trouble. Yet, of course, all that was soon to change, and though the credit for that must ultimately go to God, it was in no small part down to Ananias as well. For God's purpose to be fulfilled and for Paul's ministry to begin, it needed someone first to say yes to both. Ananias was that person.

He said yes, first, to God's challenge. 'The Lord said to him, "Get up and go to the street known as The Straight, and there look in the house of Judas for a man called Saul of Tarsus"' (Acts 9:11). As we have already seen, that challenge was enough to send a shiver down the spine of even the most fearless. It went against all reason, everything he knew of the man, so it is little wonder that his first reaction was one of doubt and incredulity. Could Paul really have changed? Does a leopard ever change its spots? How would you have felt? It would have been easy and perfectly understandable for Ananias to dismiss God's voice as autosuggestion, a figment of his imagination brought on by panic at the news Paul was in Damascus, but he didn't do that. Instead, he had the courage to believe, even when what God was saying seemed impossible; the courage to keep on listening, even when he didn't much like what he was hearing. Are we ready to say yes in turn?

If that first yes was hard, the second must have been equally so, for he was asked also to say yes to God's purpose. '[T]he Lord told him, "Go, for he is my chosen vessel through which I will make my name known before Gentiles and kings, and before the children of Israel"' (Acts 9:15). It's easy enough for us, with the benefit of hindsight, to accept and applaud the mysterious ways of God, but put yourself in the shoes of Ananias and consider how he must have felt. He knew that Saul had stood by approvingly at the stoning of Stephen and since that time had been breathing murderous threats against the Church. He knew that he had been personally involved in rooting out Christians wherever he could find them, dragging them away from their homes and families before committing them to prison. He knew he had inflicted untold misery on countless individuals, persecuting and destroying without compunction, yet here was God announcing that he had chosen

14

this same Saul to be the instrument of his purpose. Only, apparently, Paul was no longer the same person; he had changed, transformed by the grace of Christ. Would you have believed that? More important, *could* you have believed that? Would you have been able to overcome the fear, resentment, suspicion and anger that would inevitably have burned within you? Ananias did. Though he couldn't understand how it was possible, or square it with what he knew of Saul, he didn't argue but said yes to God's purpose. Are we ready to say yes in turn?

Demanding though they were, those two responses of Ananias were the easy part, for the next thing he had to do was say yes to being sent. This, if you like, was the crunch moment, the point when faith had to show itself in action rather than words. It doesn't take much, after all, to accept something if it makes no practical difference to us either way. On the other hand, if we have to stake our life on what we believe, it's a different proposition altogether, and that's what was being asked of Ananias. If he'd got things wrong about Saul, the notion of his conversion an empty delusion, then the chances were, should he go knocking on his door, that he wouldn't live to tell the tale. Reasons to put it off, to test God's call, to make doubly sure would not have been hard to find, but Ananias believed God wanted him to go, so he went. Once more, he said yes to God. Are we ready to say yes in turn?

Finally, and equally important, Ananias said yes to Saul. Here was surely the hardest thing of all. When that door was opened, and the man many feared and hated as a monster stood before him, what must have been going through Ananias' mind? How must he have felt as he entered that room and saw Saul sitting there, the man who had come to Damascus with the express purpose of destroying the Church? How would you have reacted knowing that this man had done more than any other to set back the cause of the Christian faith? Could you have looked Saul in the eye? Could you have taken him by the hand? Could you have offered him help and healing? Yet what were the words Ananias used in greeting? 'Brother Saul, the Lord has sent me – Jesus who appeared to you on your way here – in order that you may see again and be filled with the Holy Spirit' (Acts 9:17). 'Brother Saul' – of all the greetings in the New Testament, few can be more memorable than this and few have required more courage. Such was the faith of Ananias: he didn't just believe God *could* change Saul; he believed he *had*! Through saying yes to Saul, he again said yes to God. Are we ready to say yes in turn?

Are we ready to listen to God's challenge, or do we thrust it aside? Are we ready to accept his purpose rather than our own, or do we measure the world by our yardstick rather than his? Are we ready to act upon our faith, or is it all simply talk? Are we ready to reach out to others in loving acceptance, believing that God has the power to change lives, or are there those who deep down we consider beyond his grace? I cannot say what God may ask of you, any more than I know what he may one day ask of me, but I know for certain that he will ask something of all of us. Remember then the story of Ananias, and consider the fact that if he had not possessed the faith and courage to respond as he did, there might never have been a story of Saul to tell and perhaps therefore never a story of our faith too. Ananias was ready to say yes to God. Are we ready to say yes in turn?

Summary

- Such is the power of the story of Saul's conversion that we can overlook the vital contribution within it made by Ananias.
- Understandably, his initial reaction on being called to go to the house where Saul was lodging was to say no.
- Ultimately, however, Ananias had the faith to say yes.
- He said yes, first, to God's challenge. Whereas we might have refused even to consider the possibility, Ananias was ready to listen to what God was saying.
- He said yes also to God's purpose, recognising that God's ways were not his own.

- He said yes, thirdly, to acting in faith, ready to go where God sent him.
- Finally, he was ready to say yes to Paul, overcoming his natural inclinations in the conviction that God is truly able to change people.
- Have we the courage to say yes when God calls us, and yes to those he has called?

Discussion

- Had you been Ananias, what would you have found the hardest thing to accept?
- What aspects of faith do you find it easy to accept in theory but hard in practice?
- Are there times when you have felt you ought to say yes to God, but have said no? What were these and why did you respond as you did? Equally, are there times when you have said yes, and then found you have mistaken or misunderstood God's call?

Prayer

Loving God,
   there are times in our lives when you call us
   to tasks that seem beyond us,
   tasks we would rather avoid.
We hear your voice but feel unable to meet the challenge,
   our natural inclination to run away.
Remind us that when you ask us to do something,
   you give us the strength to do it.
Give us courage, then, to respond when you call,
   knowing that however things may seem,

you are always able to transform them
in ways far beyond our expectations.
Through Jesus Christ our Lord.
Amen.

Meditation of Ananias

Let's be honest, I was terrified,
    absolutely terrified.
We'd been trying to avoid him,
    hiding away for dear life,
    our hearts trembling as we waited for the thud of footsteps
    that would spell the end.
So you can imagine,
    when I felt this sudden urge to see him,
    I thought I was dreaming –
    either that or off my head!
Saul! The very name sent shivers down our spines –
    avowed enemy of the Church,
    persecutor of all who followed Christ,
    determined to wipe out every last believer.
That's why he'd come to Damascus,
    to drag us back in irons,
    and he would have shown no mercy,
    we all knew that.
Yet somehow I couldn't get that voice out of my head:
    'Go and see him!'
I tried to fight it,
    told myself it was a trick of the mind,
    but it was no good;
    I knew God was calling me.
So I went,
    and found him,
    and discovered that Jesus had found him first.

He was blind, you know,
 totally blind,
 yet he told me he had seen the light;
 that he was able to see more clearly than ever before,
 and as he spoke the tears poured down his face.
I knew what he meant, but I had my doubts at first;
 well, so would you have, wouldn't you?
I thought it was a trap,
 some cunning plan to worm his way
 into our inner circle and catch us out.
I was waiting for him to suddenly leap up,
 eyes flashing again with hatred,
 ready to devour his prey.
But it didn't happen.
When I reached out and touched him,
 finally overcoming my fear,
 he looked at me for the first time,
 and there was only love.
I still remember that day so clearly.
For one thing, I shall never forget the sheer terror
 as I stood outside his door,
 as I raised my hand to knock,
 as I set foot into the room and saw him.
But I shall never forget also
 that expression of his when his eyes were opened,
 the expression of a man who had found peace.
I'm so glad Jesus gave me the courage I needed
 to face that moment,
 the courage to say yes.
He'd accepted Paul,
 valued him
 and loved him,
 but he needed someone else to do the same.

Further reading: Hebrews 13:5b-6

He himself has categorically said, I will never abandon or forsake you, so take heart and say, 'I will not be afraid – the Lord is my helper, so what can anyone do to me?'

Suggestions for action

If there's something you've been saying no to that, deep down, you know you need to do, stop fighting against it, and say yes.

Closing prayer

Living Lord,
    when you ask me to go out in your name –
    to listen to your voice,
    to venture into the unknown,
    to let go of self and to reach out in love –
    teach me to be strong, courageous, obedient and faithful;
    teach me to say yes.
Amen.

Second week

Barnabas: Ready to encourage

Opening prayer

Lord, make me an instrument of your peace:
    where there is hatred, let me sow love;
    where there is injury, pardon;
    where there is doubt, faith;
    where there is despair, hope;
    where there is darkness, light;
    and where there is sadness, joy.
Divine Master,
    grant that I may not so much seek to be consoled as to console;
    to be understood as to understand;
    to be loved as to love.
For it is in giving that we receive,
    in pardoning that we are pardoned,
    and in dying that we are born to eternal life.
Amen.

Attributed to St Francis of Assisi

Introduction

It was heartbreaking to watch – a quality striker playing as though he had two left feet and had never seen a football in his life, making a hash of every chance that came his way. The crowd was growing impatient, not knowing whether to laugh or cry, jeering each time he got the ball and groaning in despair as yet again he blazed it high and wide. For the individual in question, it was a nightmare, his confidence visibly sapping with every game, every move, every pass. But then, a freak moment, the ball ricocheting in the penalty area as though on a pinball table, before finally bouncing off his head quite by chance and finding its way into the net. Luck it may have been, but the mood of the fans changed in an instant, and with it the attitude of the player. 'Come on!' they cried, roaring him forward, and the sudden spring in his step was unmistakable. A drop of the shoulders, sudden change of pace, and he was through, despatching the ball past the keeper with almost surgical precision. Electrifying! And now the crowd was going wild, chanting the player's name in their relief at his unexpected return to form. It was no surprise to anyone when he shimmied past three defenders as though they were not there and hammered the ball into the net to complete his hat-trick, confidence by now positively oozing from every pore!

An unlikely scenario? Don't you believe it! It's happened year after year in football grounds across the country, as legions of fickle supporters will readily testify, and it provides a graphic illustration of the role of encouragement in nurturing and maintaining confidence. When someone is constantly on your back, carping and criticising, it's hard if not impossible to give your best. By contrast, a word of praise, encouragement or inspiration can bring out potential we never even knew existed. It's easy to underestimate that gift; indeed, we may doubt that it's even a gift at all. Ask someone who has received encouragement first-hand after struggling to find their feet and questioning their ability to get through, and, believe me, they will soon tell you otherwise.

Activity

Lego® puzzle (see page 68).

Reading: Acts 4:36-37; 15:36-41

Joseph – a Levite and Cypriot, by descent – who had been nicknamed Barnabas by the Apostles, meaning 'Son of Encouragement', sold

the land that he owned and laid the proceeds at the Apostles' feet
. . . Some time later, Paul suggested to Barnabas, 'Let's pay a return
visit to every city where we have announced the word of the Lord,
to see how the believers are getting on there.' Barnabas wanted to
take John Mark with them, but Paul felt it inappropriate to take
someone who had deserted them in Pamphylia and failed to
accompany them in their work. A sharp disagreement ensued, as a
result of which they parted company; Barnabas took Mark with
him and sailed to Cyprus, while Paul, having chosen Silas, set out
on his journey, commended by the believers to the Lord's grace.
He went through Syria and Cilicia, affirming the work of the
churches there.

Comment

What sort of people help us most when we are trying to do something for the first time or wrestle with a task that we find
difficult. The answer, I suspect, is someone who encourages us. I
can well remember how at school I struggled to get to grips with
learning French, withering with embarrassment under the caustic
comments of my teacher, only for the situation to be transformed
when a new class brought a new tutor with an altogether different
approach, his gentle and patient explanations, and above all his
sense of fun, turning the subject from purgatory to a pleasure. We
will all recall similar experiences, learning perhaps to swim, ride a
bike, or drive a car, a few words of encouragement proving of
more value than all the lectures in the world.

The importance of encouragement simply cannot be exaggerated,
a fact we do well to bear in mind when we come to consider the
ministry of Barnabas, one of the many unsung heroes of the New
Testament. Like several others, he appears among the supporting
cast, frequently mentioned in the early chapters of Acts as the
right-hand man of the Apostle Paul during the first of his missionary
journeys, but then more or less disappearing from sight. However,
the little we are told of him offers eloquent testimony to the esteem

in which he was held and the contribution he made to the life of the early Church, for here was someone who exhibited the precious quality of encouraging others in abundance.

So, early in the book of Acts, we find Barnabas selling some land and offering the proceeds to the Apostles to support the work of the Church. A generous and impulsive act, but clearly one in keeping with what people already knew of this man, for the Apostles had already given him the nickname Barnabas, 'Son of Encouragement'. In other words, on more than one occasion previously Barnabas must have given heart and inspiration to those around him, perhaps, just as here, through his willingness to share what he had with others, to give what he could in the service of Christ. While others talked about sacrifice and considered how much they could give, Barnabas acted, showing his faith not just in words but deeds.

There was more, though, to Barnabas than giving – much more. A few chapters later into Acts, and we find ourselves following on from the story of Ananias in our last session. Remember how Ananias had been called to visit Saul and offer the hand of friendship? That gesture had led to Saul's acceptance in Damascus, but what of those in Jerusalem, those who had witnessed first-hand the depths to which Paul could stoop and the full extent of his hatred? Understandably, the majority were more than a little sceptical at claims he had miraculously come to faith. Could Saul (or Paul as he was to become known) really have changed, or was this some devious ploy to worm his way into the Church's inner circle, an attempt by stealth and subterfuge to infiltrate its heart and round up its ringleaders? Unlike the church in Damascus, they were unable to get past their suspicions. As the book of Acts puts it, 'they were all afraid of him, unable to believe that he was genuinely a disciple' (Acts 9:26) – all, that is, expect Barnabas, who, we read, 'took Paul, introduced him to the apostles, and told how he had encountered the Lord on the road to Damascus, and how he had boldly spoken out there in the name of Jesus' (Acts 9:27). Here was a decisive moment not just in the life of Paul but of the Church itself. All too easily, Paul could have been turned away, with who knows what repercussions, but Barnabas stepped in and spoke out on his behalf, risking his own neck and reputation for him. Through his testimony to the genuineness of Paul's conversion and the sincerity of his faith, he encouraged the Apostles to forget the past, put aside their doubts and accept Paul as one of their own. Where others saw the worst, Barnabas saw the best.

Again, though, there is more. Turn to Acts 11:22-26, and we find another way in which Barnabas was to exercise his simple ministry. News had reached the church in Jerusalem of numerous new churches springing up in Phoenicia, Cyprus and Antioch, young Christians there full of enthusiasm, bursting with newfound faith, but crying out for nurture, advice and guidance. Who was it sent to visit but Barnabas, and the reason for the choice soon becomes clear: 'When he reached there and saw evidence for himself of the grace of God, he was delighted and encouraged them all to stay faithful to the Lord with all their hearts. He was a good man, filled with the Holy Spirit and faith, and numerous people were brought to the Lord' (Acts 11:23-24). Were there, then, no problems in these churches, no difficulties to be resolved, no mistakes being made? Of course there were, and another person might all too easily have started with just those, but not Barnabas. He began with encouragement, focusing on the good and the positive, and the results speak for themselves.

Look, finally, at Acts 15:36-39, for here is yet another dimension to the gift of encouragement. An unexpected dispute had arisen between Barnabas and Paul concerning John Mark, the young man who had accompanied them on their first missionary journey, only to get cold feet and abandon the venture halfway through, no longer able to cope with the endless demands and privations. It was an understandable reaction from a young man at the end of his tether, but for Paul it was unforgivable. In his view, Mark had jeopardised their God-given mission, and he was in no mood to make allowances. Barnabas was different. Whereas Paul felt unable ever to trust Mark again, Barnabas was ready to give him a second chance, and so strongly did he feel about this that he and Paul eventually parted company after what is termed 'a sharp disagreement'. Paul went his way, choosing a new helper, Silas; Barnabas took Mark and set off for Cyprus. Which of the two was the best judge of character? I think the fact that Mark was later to write a Gospel more than answers the question. The encouragement of believing in someone, despite past failure; of seeing what *might be* rather than what *has been* – here once more is the gift of Barnabas.

'Go on supporting and encouraging each other, just as you are currently doing,' says Paul in his first letter to the Thessalonians (5:11). Were these words inspired by the example of Barnabas? I wonder. Whether they were or not, Paul had clearly grasped the importance of this ministry of encouragement, so simple, so vital, yet all too rarely learned. Furthermore, if we look at Colossians 4:11 and 1 Timothy 4:11, we find that Paul's attitude to Mark obviously mellowed, for it is clear here that he had come to value once again the part Mark continued to play in his ministry. Was this directly down to Barnabas, and the acceptance he had so unfailingly shown?

It is easier to pick holes in people than to encourage; to find fault rather than offer praise; to see weaknesses rather than strengths; and to focus on what is wrong rather than applaud what is right. It may be easy, but such a carping spirit helps no one and achieves nothing. It is through encouraging others by caring and sharing, trusting and accepting, that we help people to discover their true potential, and in so doing we have a share in the ministry of Christ. Which are you: someone who builds up or puts down, helps or hinders, encourages or discourages? It may not sound the most dramatic of gifts, but don't be fooled: a little encouragement can go a good deal further than you might ever dream. Try it, and see.

Summary

- When we're struggling with something, a word of encouragement can make all the difference between success and failure. Conversely, discouragement can cause even the best to founder.
- The gift of encouragement was recognised in Barnabas by fellow members of the early Church.

- Barnabas exercised this ministry in a variety of ways: through sharing what he had with others, helping people to overcome their doubts and fears, focusing on the positive, giving another chance and believing the best.
- It is all too easy to discourage rather than encourage, developing a negative and critical approach rather than bringing out the best in people.
- We should never underestimate what a word or gesture of encouragement can achieve. The example of Barnabas provides a lesson and challenge to us all.

Discussion

- In what ways have you been encouraged and discouraged over the years? What impact did this have upon you?
- In what ways are you able to encourage others?
- Have you been offering as much encouragement as you should? What things get in the way of us encouraging people?

Prayer

Gracious God,
    we are reminded that you call us to support one another,
    to offer comfort in times of need,
    reassurance in times of fear,
    strength in times of challenge,
    and encouragement in times of doubt.
Forgive us for so easily doing the opposite –
    for finding fault,
    running down,
    criticising and condemning.
Forgive us for seeing the worst instead of the best,
    for believing the bad instead of the good,

for so often pulling down and so rarely building up.
Teach us to recognise people's gifts and nurture them,
    to understand their problems and share them,
    to acknowledge their successes and applaud them,
    to appreciate their efforts and affirm them.
Teach us, through the faith we show in people,
    to help them attempt great things and expect great things,
    to look at life seeing not the obstacles but the opportunities,
    not the things they can't do but the things they can.
So may we help them to believe in themselves,
    to discover their abilities,
    to appreciate their worth,
    and to fulfil their potential.
Through Jesus Christ our Lord.
Amen.

Meditation of Barnabas

It wasn't much of a gift,
    at least I didn't think so.
In fact, I didn't feel I had a gift at all,
    not like the rest of them with their stunning signs and wonders.
I envied them sometimes,
    so often in the limelight,
    stealing all the headlines –
    prophets,
    teachers,
    workers of miracles,
    speakers of tongues.
They were the ones who drew the crowds,
    the ones people noticed,
    while all I did was plod quietly along,
    living the faith in my own simple way,
    speaking and doing,
    caring and sharing,

as I believed Christ would have me do.
And then they gave me this name –
    Barnabas,
    'Son of Encouragement'.
It was a complete surprise,
    for what had I done to deserve any such honour?
But then they told me,
    one by one,
    that of all the gifts they valued,
    mine was chief among them.
A generous gesture,
    a word of praise,
    an expression of trust,
    a sign of love –
    not causing gasps,
    not making heads turn,
    yet these, they told me, had stirred their hearts
    and cheered their spirits
    as signs and wonders could never do.
It doesn't seem much does it –
    encouraging people –
    hardly the sort of gift people will fight over,
    yet don't let that fool you as it did me.
If you're wondering, as I did, why you've been left out,
    waiting for the Spirit and perplexed he hasn't come,
    let me offer you some simple words of encouragement:
    follow Jesus,
    faithfully and simply,
    for it's often when you're least aware of it,
    through things you count least important,
    that he chooses to use you
    and that his Spirit is most powerfully at work.

Further reading: Hebrews 10:24-25

Let us consider how we might spur each other on in love and good works, not forgetting to meet together, as some have grown accustomed to doing; but encouraging one another, and doing so increasingly as we see the Day approaching.

Suggestions for action

When you find a negative comment or destructive criticism forming on your lips, bite your tongue and think again. Ask yourself if there is something positive and helpful you can say instead. Set yourself a target of encouraging people in whatever way you are able.

Closing prayer

Loving God,
   as you encourage us,
   so may we encourage others,
   through Jesus Christ our Lord.
Amen.

Third week

James: Ready to listen

Opening prayer

Gracious Father, we pray for your Christian Church.
Fill it with all truth, and in all truth with all peace.
Where it is corrupt, cleanse it.
Where it is in error, direct it.
Where it is superstitious, rectify it.
Where anything is amiss, reform it.
Where it is right, strengthen and confirm it.
Where it is in want, supply its need.
Where it is divided and torn apart, heal the divisions,
O holy one of Israel,
    for the sake of Jesus Christ our Lord and Saviour.
Amen.

Archbishop William Laud

Introduction

There is a trend in some quarters of the Church today that I find
deeply disturbing. I refer to the underlying assumption that a simple
and unequivocal Christian stance can be taken on any and every
moral issue. In issues as complex as sexuality, contraception, abortion
and euthanasia, there are those who tell us that there can only be one
Christian response, anyone who suggests otherwise being dismissed
as theologically unsound. Similarly short shrift is given to any
idea that there needs to be informed debate on biblical teaching or
that it may need to be interpreted in the light of modern research. I
can understand why people feel this way, for many are genuinely
alarmed by what they see as the decline in moral standards within

contemporary Western society. Without question, open-mindedness isn't always the quality it's cracked up to be, often synonymous with an attitude of 'anything goes'. Those who suggest there are moral and ethical frontiers beyond which it is wrong to venture are dismissed as bigoted, blinkered and out of touch with reality. In other words, intolerance can usually be found on both sides of an argument, and the result is that each tends to harden their position rather than listen to what the other is saying. The story of James helps us to understand that open-mindedness doesn't necessarily mean that we accept everything, but rather that we are ready to give a fair hearing to another's point of view, amenable to the possibility that we may need to reconsider our opinions in the light of their experience. His willingness to listen opened the way for the Christian faith to spread across the Roman world. Had his mind been closed, the young Church may instead have turned in on itself in suspicion, prejudice and infighting. As individuals and as Christians today, we need a similar openness to the possibility that truth may be wider than we have ever begun to imagine.

Activity

Listen carefully (see page 69).

1) *Start here*

Reading: Acts 15:1-2, 12-20

Then certain individuals came down from Judea and were teaching the brothers, 'Unless you are circumcised according to the custom of Moses, you cannot be saved.' And after Paul and Barnabas had no small dissension and debate with them, Paul and Barnabas and some of the others were appointed to go up to Jerusalem to discuss this question with the apostles and the elders. The whole assembly kept silence, and listened to Barnabas and Paul as they told of all the signs and wonders that God had done through them among the Gentiles. After they finished speaking, James replied, 'My brothers, listen to me. Simeon has related how God first looked favourably on the Gentiles, to take from among them a people for his name. This agrees with the words of the prophets, as it is written, "After this I will return, and I will rebuild the dwelling of David, which has fallen; from its ruins I will rebuild it, and I will set it up, so that all other peoples may seek the Lord – even all the Gentiles over whom my name has been called. Thus says the Lord, who has been making these things known from long ago." Therefore I have reached the decision that we should not trouble those Gentiles who are turning to God, but we should write to them to abstain only from things polluted by idols and from fornication and from whatever has been strangled and from blood.' (*NRSV*)

Comment

It is often said that there are two sides to every coin, and that truth powerfully emerges in the story of James. We talk, don't we, of sticking up for our principles, being certain of what we believe, but is that right or wrong? As always, there is a thin line between what is good and bad, a vice or a virtue! Firm principles and unwavering belief can very easily transmute into entrenched and unyielding narrow-mindedness, an inflexible dogmatic insistence on the rightness of one's own views at the expense of all others. We need the courage of our convictions, yes, but we must also be ready to have some of those convictions challenged and examined, even if that means modifying or abandoning altogether beliefs long held dear. So it was to prove in the case of James.

There is some debate as to who James actually was, but the most widely accepted view is that he was none other than the brother of Jesus: a Jew through and through, steeped in Jewish tradition and custom. Understandably, then, he held his Jewish heritage dear, notwithstanding his faith in Christ. For him, Christianity was not something revolutionary, breaking away from the past, but the fulfilment of Old Testament prophecy and the realisation of

33

everything his people had longed for across the centuries. If the gospel was for all, Gentile as well as Jew, the implications of what that might mean had scarcely begun to dawn on him or on the early Church. Yet the comfortable *status quo* was soon to be rudely shaken as news of the missionary work of Paul filtered back to Jerusalem, including stories of Gentiles admitted into the Church without any of the requirements of the Law being placed upon them. If some were willing to turn a blind eye, others were not, such an unconditional welcome seeming to strike at the very fabric of their faith. Did Gentiles have a share in the promises of God? Could they too receive the blessing of Christ and the gift of his Spirit? According to the sceptics, this could only be so if Gentiles first became adoptive Jews, accepting and acknowledging the various prescriptions and proscriptions of the Jewish Law – rules concerning circumcision, food that had been consecrated to idols, and a host of other ceremonial and ritual regulations.

Here was a controversy that threatened to tear the Church apart while it was still barely in its infancy. On both sides, tempers were frayed and debate increasingly acidic, Jews adamant that the Law must not be compromised, with Gentiles equally insistent that its stipulations could not and should not apply to them. It was imperative that the matter was brought to a head, and so a special Council was called in Jerusalem to debate the matter, at which the main speakers were James representing the standpoint of the Jews, and Peter, Barnabas and Paul pleading the case of the Gentiles. For many, there could be only one outcome of this meeting: a gentle but firm reprimand that would put Paul in his place, reminding him of his roots and his need to honour them. The result, though, was to be very different.

After Peter, Barnabas and Paul had finished speaking, James replied, 'My brothers, listen to me. Simeon [Peter] has related how God first looked favourably on the Gentiles, to take from among them a people for his name. This agrees with the words of the prophets . . . Therefore I have reached the decision that we should not trouble those Gentiles who are turning to God' (Acts 15:13-15, 19, *NRSV*). The key detail here lies in those opening words: '*When they had finished*, James spoke up.' In other words, before he spoke, James listened. Unlike the majority, he had not made up his mind before discussion started, or at least, if he had, he was not totally closed to any possibility of change! He heard what Peter, Paul and Barnabas had to say with an open mind, only reaching a conclusion when he had listened to all the arguments and weighed them in the balance; a conclusion based not on prejudice or predetermined assumptions but on the evidence placed before him of what God had done and was doing.

His decision, though, was not simply based on his own assessment of the issues, or the force of any single line of reasoning. He was anxious to seek God's will rather than his own or someone else's, and so he measured what others had said against what he believed God was saying concerning the issue. For him, confirmation seemed to come in the words of the prophets, and particularly of the prophet Amos, whose words were being fulfilled in a new and exciting way: 'all other peoples may seek the Lord – even all the Gentiles over whom my name has been called. Thus says the Lord, who has been making these things known from long ago' (Acts 15:17, *NRSV*).

Open to others and open to God – it was this that led James to welcome Gentiles with the least demands possible, and this that was ultimately to transform a small Jewish sect into a world-changing faith crossing the boundaries of race, colour and culture, and every other boundary imaginable. Instead of frustrating the Spirit and stifling the message of the gospel, both were set free to realise their full potential. It is extraordinary to think that without his courage and honesty the Christian faith might have died a death back in Jerusalem; that you and I might have heard nothing of Christ, and the Church might barely have started before it was finished. Through one individual's open-mindedness and willingness to listen, new horizons were opened!

All this is not to say, of course, that the problem was dealt with overnight. You'd be highly sceptical if an issue as divisive as this could be settled in one discussion in such a way that everyone lived happily ever after, and you'd have every reason to be so.

Human nature just isn't like that, for there are always some who find it hard to change and others who refuse to bend, come what may. So Paul was to be dogged throughout his ministry by those who insisted, despite everything, that Gentiles must observe the letter of the Law, their dogmatic stance often spilling over into outright hostility. Nor should we assume that agreement on welcoming the Gentiles meant a uniformity of opinion and practice that could be rigidly imposed. As Paul was to write later to the Galatians: 'when James, Cephas and John, who were acknowledged pillars, recognised the grace that had been given to me, they gave to Barnabas and me the right hand of fellowship, agreeing that we should go to the Gentiles and they to the circumcised' (Galatians 2:9; *NRSV*). In other words, there was room for accommodation on both sides, an acceptance that truth can have more than one face.

It is hard to admit we are wrong or to accept ideas that differ from our own. Sadly, that has sometimes seemed hardest of all within the Church; the more an opinion or belief means to us, the more inclined we are to defend it at all costs. If you doubt that, you need only look at the repeated instances of religious persecution and intolerance across the years, and the tensions that continue to scar many parts of our world today. Not that the problem is simply out there, concerned with others. We may like to think we are more open-minded than most, ready to listen and give a fair hearing to other points of view, but we all have ingrained prejudices that we find it hard to identify, let alone overcome. Within society as a whole, issues of race, religion, gender, sex and politics are but a few of the areas in which opinions can still be entrenched. Within the Church, questions relating to worship, tradition, theology and church practice can be equally divisive. Whether it is new ideas or different ways of thinking, conflicting understandings or contrasting emphases, we must learn, like James, to listen with open minds, and then to measure what we hear against what God is saying, recognising that he is bigger than any one person's grasp of truth.

James, like all of those in this book, flits but briefly across the New Testament stage, but in doing so he poses a challenge we cannot afford to ignore. Are we open to others and open to God?

Only then can he carry us forward into a richer and deeper understanding of truth.

Summary

- Sticking to our principles can in reality be nothing more than pigheadedness.
- The early Church had to face up to controversy surrounding the admission of Gentiles into the Church; a controversy that involved matters of principle on both sides.
- James, as head of the Jerusalem church, was called on to hear the evidence and mediate between the two parties.
- The first thing James did, before coming to a decision, was listen to the contrasting points of view, including that which differed to the one he had grown up with.
- Having listened, he measured what he had heard against God's word, allowing that to be the final arbiter.
- Through his willingness to listen with an open mind, James opened the way for Christianity to break down barriers throughout the world.
- Reaching accord, however, was not entirely straightforward, nor did it result in everyone thinking or acting in exactly the same way.
- Admitting we are wrong or accepting other points of view is not easy. Christians can find it as hard as any, if not harder. To adapt or even alter our beliefs can be too painful to contemplate. The history of the Church powerfully illustrates the point.
- All of us are more entrenched in our ideas than we may think. Numerous issues continue to divide both society in general and the Church.
- Are we willing to listen to others and to God, open to the possibility that what they have to say may lead us into a deeper understanding of truth? *Learning about other Christian churches & other faiths*

Problem areas for christians — War, the death penalty, birth control, private schools & hospitals, smoking, DRINK, Christian unity, attitude to the Bible, women priests, styles of worship, church music, Sabbath observe

Discussion

- Are there blind spots in your mind, areas where you find it hard to be open to new ideas and insights? What are these, what causes them, and why do you find it hard to break them down?

- How many problems in contemporary society have their roots in a failure to see another person or group's point of view?

- What qualities are needed for genuine dialogue?

- Is there a danger of using Scripture as a way of defending closed attitudes rather than being open to God's voice?

- Can Christians genuinely be open, given that they hold certain underlying and unshakable beliefs?

Also the Jews, attitudes to Divorce

Prayer

Gracious God,
 you speak to us in all kinds of ways
 and through all kinds of people –
 yet sometimes we are closed to what you would say.
We avoid those things that challenge or unsettle us,
 preferring to pick holes and nitpick over trivialities
 rather than face up to complex issues.
We are reluctant to accept new and unfamiliar ideas,
 taking refuge instead in what is tried and trusted.
We resent opinions that contradict our own,
 shutting our ears to what we don't agree with
 rather than listen to another point of view.
Forgive us,
 and break through the barriers we erect against you,
 so that we may hear your voice,
 know your truth,
 and live as your people,
 to the glory of your name.
Amen.

Meditation of James

Gentiles!
In *our* Church?
No thank you.
Oh, you may frown,
    shake your head in disapproval,
    but remember this:
    we were Jews,
    steeped in tradition,
    brought up to see the world in terms of them and us,
    clean and unclean –
    so how else could you expect us to feel?
Anyway, give us credit,
    we weren't closed altogether –
    if folk wanted to join us, fair enough,
    but let them first adopt *our* ways,
    our customs,
    our Law,
    and then apply –
    you can't argue with that, can you?
Only, apparently, some did,
    and chief among them – can you believe it? – was Paul.
I was stunned at the time –
    him of all people:
    schooled as a Pharisee,
    zealous in the Law,
    and one-time sworn enemy of Christ –
    yet there he was,
    preaching the gospel among them,
    demanding there be no conditions,
    no strings attached –
    open admission to all.
Frankly, I was appalled,
    quite certain that nothing and no one
    would ever change my position,

but I couldn't have been more wrong;
from the moment he started to speak,
the truth was staring me in the face,
impossible to resist.
No, it wasn't all sweetness and light, don't think that.
We had our moments, like anyone else,
and there were some on both sides pushing for more concessions,
a tougher line,
unable to bring themselves to bend.
But for most of us, when we heard what God was doing –
how lives were being changed,
faith born,
the Spirit released –
there could be no arguing.
It wasn't down to me
or Paul
or anyone else.
God was working his purpose out
with or without us –
far better to be on board,
nurturing his kingdom rather than conspiring against it.
I'm not saying we've got things sorted,
not by a long way,
for there are still some not happy,
complex, controversial issues yet to be resolved,
but I tell you this: it's no use digging in,
closing your ears,
convincing yourself that *you're* right and others are wrong.
You may safeguard your principles, that way,
protect your little kingdom,
but if *God's* kingdom turns out
other than you've bargained on,
don't be surprised that you failed to see the truth,
for the fact is you never stopped to look.

Further reading: 1 Corinthians 4:5a

Judge nothing prematurely, before the Lord returns, for he will shed light on those things hidden in darkness and reveal the innermost thoughts of people's hearts.

Suggestions for action

Examine those convictions you feel strongly about, especially those you may have been brought up to accept without question. Find out more about the contrasting positions and ask yourself whether you need to revise your own views in the light of them.

Closing prayer

God of all,
    break through the barriers that shut our minds fast,
    and help us to see things both as they really are
    and as you can help them become.
Move within us,
    and open our eyes to truth,
    wherever you would speak it,
    in the name of Christ.
Amen.

Fourth week

Epaphras: Ready to pray

Prayer

In me, my God, be present,
  be always here.
And may you find your home in me,
  just as you are, my God.
Amen.

Carmelite Monastery, Quidenham

Introduction

'I'll pray for you.' How often have you promised to do that, and
how often have you failed? It's not that we don't mean what we
say; simply that other things get in the way so that the promise
slips our mind. Contrast that with the tribute paid by Paul to the
man in those verses below: Epaphras, someone who was 'always
wrestling in prayer'. How many would say that of us, I wonder?
We may very possibly wrestle with the concept or discipline of
prayer, but probably few of us could be said to wrestle *in* prayer.
Epaphras was someone who didn't just *talk* about prayer but
practised it, to the point that his commitment was unmistakable.
Equally important, though, as we shall see, there was more to
his prayer-life than words alone, for this man was no ascetic or
spiritual recluse. Could we only know more about him, I suspect
he would have much to teach us about what Paul meant in his
injunction to the Thessalonians to 'pray at all times without ceasing'
(1 Thessalonians 5:16); a call I explore in more detail in another
book in this series, *Prayer – the fundamental questions*. What is clear,
however, is that Epaphras could honestly say, 'I'll pray for you',
because he really meant it. How many of us can say the same?

Activity

Arm wrestling (see page 69).

Reading: Colossians 4:12

Epaphras, from among your number and a servant of Jesus Christ, sends greetings. He is always wrestling on your behalf in prayer, asking that you may stand firm, mature and fully assured of the will of God.

Comment

How often do you make time for prayer? Once or twice a day, perhaps? Maybe even three times? Or is the reality more like once a week? Consider, then, if you will, the following programme: an hour's prayer at three in the morning; up again at six and again at nine for a repeat performance; then further prayers at noon, three in the afternoon, six and nine in the evening, and a final burst at midnight, just to round things off. How do you fancy that? Not very much? Well, to be honest, neither do I. A few may be called to the monastic way of life, but most of us would find such a discipline of prayer impossible to maintain, even if we felt it desirable. Quite simply, life has too much else to offer, and puts too many demands upon us, for us to devote more than a short time each day to prayer, at least in the formal sense of the word.

A cursory look at the verse of our reading above might suggest that Epaphras, as someone 'always wrestling in prayer', was of the monastic ilk, but a fuller inspection of the New Testament reveals otherwise. There is much else, as well as prayer, for which Epaphras might justifiably be remembered. For example, like Paul, he was to be imprisoned for his faith; indeed, as we read in Philemon 23, for a time he was one of Paul's fellow-prisoners. Again like Paul, he was someone who served in the work of mission, proclaiming the gospel in word and deed, and making a significant contribution to the growth of the Church. Almost certainly, it was Epaphras who helped to found the church at Colossae, Paul writing in his letter to them, 'All over the world this gospel is bearing fruit and growing, just as it has been doing among you since the day you heard it and understood God's grace in all its truth. You learned it from Epaphras, our dear fellow servant, who is a faithful minister of Christ on our behalf, and who also told us of your love in the Spirit' (Colossians 1:6-8, *NIV*). Epaphras, then, was a person of considerable gifts, who clearly did much in the early years of the Church to further the cause of Christ.

Yet, important though such gifts were, it was the quality mentioned earlier that inspired Paul's most fulsome tribute to his friend and fellow worker: 'Epaphras, who is one of you and a servant of Christ Jesus, sends greetings. He is always wrestling in prayer for you, that you may stand firm in all the will of God, mature and fully assured' (Colossians 4:12, *NIV*). Of all his gifts, his dedication in prayer was what, in Paul's opinion, made Epaphras stand out. In this lay his distinctive contribution to the life of the Church. In this lay the special quality of his ministry that set him apart and won the admiration and respect of his peers; the fact that he was genuinely a man of prayer. Yet, though that sounds impressive, we need to ask ourselves what it means, and, more specifically, what we can learn from his example for today.

The first thing to note is this: that, for Epaphras, prayer was an ongoing commitment rather than occasional pursuit. He didn't just indulge himself as the mood took him, fitting prayer into those odd moments when he could find a space amid more pressing concerns. It was part of his life, a privilege and responsibility. Above all, it was a priority, the one thing he would make time for before all else. The Greek word Paul uses here, αγωνιζομενος, derives from the word αγωνια, used of Jesus as he prayed in Gethsemane in the hours leading up to his death (Luke 22:44). It means to agonise, struggle, contend, strive, and the idea clearly being conveyed is that the prayers of Epaphras were from the heart: intense, purposeful, urgent and determined. Whatever else might be sacrificed, squeezed out by other demands and responsibilities, prayer would not.

Second, Epaphras prayed with a purpose. He didn't just breeze through a quick 'God bless the Church, the sick and the world'. He didn't, so far as we know, pray parrot-fashion, mechanically reciting the same words day after day until they became more a matter of habit than genuine devotion. Nor, unless I'm much mistaken, did he simply pray generally for the people of Colossae, or wherever else he was praying for, and then leave it to God to work out what exactly was needed. He evidently knew who and what he was praying for, and, equally important, why he was praying. Prayer was about concrete people and situations, not a vague and aimless consecration of the needs of the world.

Third, and following from that, Epaphras prayed for others as much as himself. That may seem so obvious that it hardly needs saying, but it's important, for all too easily prayer can become self-centred, concerned only with ourselves – our own needs and problems, faults and failings – or perhaps, if we're lucky, with our families, friends and loved ones. I have no doubt that Epaphras often prayed for himself and those closest to him – he'd have been less than human if he hadn't – but it seems likely from Paul's testimony that he prayed equally, if not more, for a wider circle – the churches in Colossae, Laodicea and Hierapolis in whose work and life he had shared. He couldn't be with them in person, but he could pray, and that's what he did, interceding faithfully on their behalf.

Finally, one other thing emerges from Paul's commendation, a detail that is arguably the most important of all. 'I can personally testify,' writes Paul, 'that he works tirelessly, both for you and for those in Laodicea and Hierapolis' (Colossians 4:12). In other words, Epaphras didn't only pray but also acted on his prayers. In what way, we are not told, but clearly there was more to his prayer-life than simply words. Perhaps he pleaded for financial help from other Christians; perhaps he fulfilled errands people had asked him to undertake; perhaps he made time regularly to visit them in order to nurture and encourage their faith. Whatever it was,

Epaphras was hard at work, turning words into deeds, making his prayers real, recognising that if they were to be answered, then it depended at least in part on him and his own response! Am I making too much of this detail? I don't think so. Without this practical side to his prayers, the other side would be devalued, if not negated altogether. Epaphras didn't just express fine sentiments and then leave everything to God. He played his part in ensuring his prayers were answered.

What, then, of us? Do we make prayer a priority in our lives, recognising it as the lifeblood of a healthy and thriving faith? Do we pray meaningfully, clear as to the purpose rather than out of a sense of duty or habit? Do we make time to pray for others as well as ourselves, and do we act to answer our prayers, backing up our words with deeds? In short, are we a people who wrestle in prayer?

Summary

- Prayer, for most of us, is something that we have to fit into the busy schedule of our lives.
- Although Epaphras is described as a man 'always wrestling in prayer', he was clearly involved in much else during his life and ministry. He did not spend all his time praying, in the sense we usually understand the word.
- Despite this, Paul clearly thought of Epaphras as a person of prayer.
- The word translated as 'wrestling' has the same root as the word used to describe the agony of Jesus as he wrestled with prayer in the garden of Gethsemane. In other words, prayer was something Epaphras took very seriously, giving it priority in his life.
- His prayers were not aimless or mechanical. He knew what he was praying for and why.
- Equally, his prayers were not all about himself or those closest to him. He made time to pray for others.

- Prayer, however, was not simply a matter of words for Epaphras. With God's help, and so far as it was within his power, he strove to answer his own prayers, acting upon his words whenever and wherever he was able.
- How far are those characteristics of prayer evident in our lives? In what sense, if any, can we call ourselves a people of prayer?

Discussion

- In what ways have you ever wrestled in prayer? What do *you* think Paul means by this? What do you find hardest about doing the same?
- Do you think prayer can be an excuse for inaction? In what way?
- How easy is it to pray with a purpose? Is it possible to pray meaningfully for people who are simply names to us? Do we sometimes spread the net too wide to pray meaningfully? Equally, do we sometimes spread it too narrowly?

Prayer

Loving God,
    forgive us that though we talk much about prayer,
    we are weak when it comes to praying,
    and weaker still in turning prayers into action.
Forgive us our neglect of prayer,
    our reluctance to take it seriously or to devote time to you.
Forgive us our empty or half-hearted prayers,
    offered more out of duty or habit than serious intent.
Teach us what it means to wrestle in prayer
    and what it means to act upon our words,
    and so may we pray always to your glory
    in the name of Christ.
Amen.

Meditation of a member of the church in Colossae

I'll pray for you, he told us,
    and we nodded, almost absent-mindedly,
    grateful,
    but scarcely taking it in.
We'd heard it often enough, you see,
    well-intentioned,
    sincerely meant,
    yet all too often simply words,
    easily spoken,
    soon forgotten.
Only this time it wasn't like that,
    for he did just what he promised,
    day after day,
    week after week,
    year after year.
Whether it was our hopes or fears,
    triumphs or tribulations,
    we knew he was always there,
    wrestling for us before God,
    sharing our dreams and disappointments
    our joys and sorrows,
    and committing them all in prayer.
It didn't just end there, though,
    in fine words and pious sentiments.
He acted on what he said,
    each prayer translated into deeds,
    answered, as far as possible, through his own service,
    his own faithful and loving response.
It was humbling to see it,
    the way he worked so tirelessly both for us and others,
    no sacrifice too large, no need too small,
    prayer not something he played at,
    but that he applied each moment –
    a way of life.

He's one in a million, of course,
    not many around like Epaphras,
    and we all realise we've been lucky to know him,
    privileged to enjoy the support he's given.
Privileged,
    but also challenged,
    his example pricking our conscience every day,
    for unlike me,
    and unlike most of us,
    he said those so familiar words, 'I'll pray for you',
    and he meant them!

Further reading: Colossians 4:2

Persevere in prayer, remaining constantly alert in it with thanksgiving.

Suggestions for action

Have you promised to pray for someone but done nothing about it? If so, need I say more!

Closing prayer

Living God,
    grant that not only my words
    but everything I am and do
    may be offered to you as a living prayer,
    in the name of Christ.
Amen.

Fifth week

Epaphroditus: Ready to drop

Opening prayer

Eternal God and Father,
  you create us by your power
  and redeem us by your love.
Guide and strengthen us by your Spirit,
  that we may give ourselves in love and service
  to one another and to you.
Through Jesus Christ our Lord.
Amen.

Daily Office Revised

Introduction

It's sometimes claimed that 'sorry' is the hardest word to say. That's probably true, but there's another word that must run it a close second – namely, the word 'no'. You may find that hard to believe, pointing to all kinds of occasions when you've appealed for help and support and none has been forthcoming, and in this sense you'd be quite right. Put out a general request for help or a plea for volunteers, and it's very likely that your appeal will fall on deaf ears. Put people on the spot, however, and reactions will swiftly change. You may still not receive an assent, but I doubt you'll get an outright refusal either. More likely you'll be greeted by something noncommittal: a promise to think about it or a tentative 'maybe' in the hope that you'll forget your request in the meantime. Most people will wriggle off the hook somehow, ensuring that they steer well clear of you until the coast is clear, but there are some people who simply find it impossible to say no. You know the sort I'm referring to – the lynchpins of many a church, club, society or organisation without whom, metaphorically speaking, the whole edifice would come tumbling down. They may be the leader at the front whose drive and energy keeps the group ticking over. They may be one of those working behind the scenes, working tirelessly in the kitchen, cleaning and maintaining the premises, or serving on every committee and post imaginable. A few may subconsciously be creating their own little empire, but most offer such service out of genuine dedication to the cause. They do so without complaining and without expecting any reward other than the satisfaction their work brings them, but, like anyone else, they can end up doing too much, perhaps only realising the danger when it's too late. Some, in fact, may be crying out for someone else to share the load, and even want to let go of their responsibilities altogether, but for a variety of reasons may feel unable to walk away. This session explores the danger of overdoing things, of saying yes when we ought to say no. At the same time, it looks at the other side of the coin: the possibility that some may be doing too much because *we* are doing too little. As you consider the story of Epaphroditus, ask yourself honestly which of those two possibilities most applies to you.

Activity

One load too many? (see page 69).

Reading: Philippians 2:25-30

I deemed it necessary to send to you Epaphroditus – my brother, co-worker and fellow-soldier, and your messenger sent to minister to me in my need – since he has been pining for you all and troubled that you heard about his illness. He was indeed so ill that he came close to death, but God had mercy on him, and not only him but me also, sparing me yet another sorrow. I therefore readily sent him to you, so that you may rejoice at seeing him again and I may be less anxious. Welcome him, then, in the Lord with all joy, and treat such as him with respect, because he risked his life for the work of Christ and came close to death in order to offer those services to me that you were unable to provide.

Comment

Who was the most popular character in the days of the early Church? It's an impossible question to answer, of course, but I suspect right up there among the best of them would have been the person I've devoted this session to, Epaphroditus. A surprising choice, you may think, for he's hardly the most renowned of individuals; indeed, it may well be that this is the first time you've ever heard of him. So what made Epaphroditus so special? The answer may surprise you still further, for his greatest strength was also his greatest weakness and very nearly his undoing. Epaphroditus, unless I'm much mistaken, was the sort of person we all like to have around; someone who was ready to say yes when others said no. You know just the type I mean: the kind of individual who, when a request is made for volunteers and you immediately look away, studiously avoiding people's gaze, suddenly pipes up with those magic words, 'All right, I'll do it'. The kind who, when others melt into the shadows, you can depend on to be there, ready to shoulder not only their load but everyone else's as well. It may be a cliché, but the old saying is true nonetheless: 'If you want a job done, ask a busy person.' Whether it is church, a club or anything else, most jobs tend to be done by the same few people while the majority do little if anything.

Such a person, I suspect, was Epaphroditus. As a member of the church in Philippi, he must already have had his fair share of commitments, but he was soon to find himself taking on many more. It started with news that the Apostle Paul was going through hard times, in need of practical as well as financial support, and above all longing for someone to visit him in prison to offer much-needed encouragement. You can well imagine the scene as that request was brought before the church in Philippi: a general nodding of heads, murmurs of sympathy and concern, and agreement all round that something had to be done, the sooner the better. Only then it came to the crunch: who would go? Would anyone be willing to give up their time and face the rigours of the journey to Rome? Was anyone prepared to share in Paul's privations, even, if necessary, risk their own safety for his sake? A long awkward silence . . . an embarrassed cough . . . a sea of uneasy faces dreading the fateful question, 'What about you?' . . . a roomful of averted eyes . . . furtive embarrassed glances to see if anyone might yet let them off the hook . . . and then suddenly those oh so welcome words: 'Well, if no one else wants to, I'll do it.' Who's speaking? Good old Epaphroditus, of course.

Am I reading too much into things? I may be, for there's no way of knowing what actually happened, yet, reading between the lines, it seems a plausible scenario, for Epaphroditus was clearly one of those people ready to do their fair share and far more besides. So it was that, when he arrived in Rome, it wasn't simply to pay Paul a token visit – to hand out a few goodies, assure him of the Philippians' concern, and then hurry off home. On the contrary, he appears to have thrown himself heart and soul into the work that Paul had previously been doing and would still have been involved in but for his chains, so much so that Paul refers to him not simply as a messenger but as 'my brother, co-worker and fellow-soldier'. A glowing tribute indeed to a man who evidently went much further than was either asked or expected of him. Yet there was a price to pay, for somehow, before he knew it, he found himself laid up in bed, fighting for his life, sick to the point of death. Was this some mystery virus or dreadful disease? Again, details are sketchy, to say the least, but the view of most commentators is that what Epaphroditus was suffering from was almost certainly a nervous breakdown brought on by sheer exhaustion – a physical and mental collapse triggered by having done too much. True or otherwise, the danger was real enough, as it is equally real for us today, and it is a danger that prompts two important questions.

First: *are you doing too much*? Are you, like Epaphroditus, one of those who takes on ever more jobs, responsibilities and demands, even when you're already flagging under the strain of others? Are you the sort who feels embarrassed and guilty at turning down a request for help? Above all, are you in danger of pushing yourself beyond the limit? You may not think so. Indeed, you may shrug aside any suggestion of overdoing things, convinced that you have the reserves to keep going come what may. But are you being realistic? The fact is that we all need a break sometimes, whoever we are. Exhaustion is something that can steal up on us unnoticed, catching us unawares. All too often, we don't recognise it until it is upon us, by which time it may be too late to undo the damage. Remember also that for many it is not simply a question of us alone paying the price, but our partner, our children, our families and friends as well. It may be, of course, that we are aware of the problem, recognising the need to ease off but feeling unable to do so. Perhaps we know that a job won't be done unless we do it; perhaps we consider it to be so important that we have to take a chance, never mind the risks; or perhaps we genuinely feel that we are more suited for a particular task than anyone else. Surely that changes things? Well, no, not if it ends up as the straw that breaks the camel's back, for then, far from doing it all, you'll end up doing nothing.

On the other hand, it may be you need to ask yourself a very different question: namely, *am I doing enough?* Are there jobs to be done that you have the time, skill and resources to undertake, but not the will? Are there tasks relating to the life of your church that you have the talents to tackle, but not the inclination? When you sit in a church meeting and someone asks for volunteers, when a post comes up for election, when an appeal is made for workers, do you seriously consider whether you can help or do you start thinking of excuses, reasons why you are unsuitable? As members of the Church, but also simply as Christians, we have a responsibility towards one another and towards God. We must all ensure, to the best of our ability, that no one is doing too much because we are doing too little.

Are you doing too much? Are you doing enough? Those are the two simple questions the story of Epaphroditus asks of us all. No one but us can answer those questions. It may be tempting to say no when our help is sought, but are we letting God down in doing so, as well as others and ourselves? It may seem the Christian thing sometimes to say yes, but if that causes our health to suffer, endangering the happiness of our loved ones and preventing us from properly fulfilling our responsibilities, then perhaps it's time we learnt to say no. All of us can do something; none of us is called to do everything.

Summary

- Epaphroditus seems to have been the sort of person who was always willing to do that bit extra; to take on a job or responsibility that no one else wanted to tackle.
- When news of Paul's imprisonment in Rome reached the ears of the church in Philippi, it was Epaphroditus who volunteered to visit him and minister to his needs.
- When he arrived in Rome, Epaphroditus clearly did more than simply visit Paul. It looks as though he also took on much of the work Paul had been involved in, for Paul describes him in his letter as a 'co-worker and fellow-soldier'.
- Because of his efforts, Epaphroditus suffered what appears to have been some kind of breakdown, brought on by sheer exhaustion, a condition that brought him close to death.
- His story poses two questions for us today. Are we doing too much or too little? Have we taken on more jobs than we are capable of doing, at risk to our own well-being and potentially that of our loved ones? Equally, are we failing to pull our weight, causing other people as a result to take on more than they should

be doing? Are we failing in our responsibilities towards God and others?

- Only we can answer such questions, no one else. Which are we? Is it time we learnt to say no or learnt to say yes?

Discussion

- Have you taken on too much or accepted responsibilities that you are unable to fulfil?
- Have you made the opposite mistake and failed to take on enough?
- Is there something you are being asked to do that you should politely but firmly refuse?
- Is there a danger of getting so sucked into the life of the Church and 'Christian' service, that you neglect your family and yourself? What do you see as the principal dangers of doing too much?

Prayer

Living God,
    it is hard sometimes to say no.
We do not want to let people down,
    especially when we have the ability to do what they ask.
We like to appear on top of things,
    capable of meeting every challenge,
    and we are reluctant to admit our limitations.
We are afraid of being thought mean or selfish
    or unwilling to put ourselves out on another's behalf.
For a whole variety of reasons,
    we find it easier sometimes to say yes than no
    even when we know in our heart
    that it is the wrong answer to give.

Teach us that there are times when we owe it to ourselves,
 our families
 or our friends
 to say no,
 and that there are times also when saying yes
 will mean that a job is not done properly, if at all.
Help us to do what we can,
 both in your service and in the service of others,
 but to recognise also what we can't do,
 and then grant us the wisdom and courage we need to say no.
In Christ's name we pray.
Amen.

Meditation of Epaphroditus

I should have said no, I realise that now,
 not just for my sake but for theirs too,
 for I was no use to anyone the way I ended up –
 just about all in,
 battered in mind and body,
 as near to death's door as I could possibly get
 without crossing the Rubicon altogether.
The trouble was I just couldn't refuse,
 my head saying one thing,
 my heart another.
Was it just loyalty, you ask,
 a desire not to let people down or leave them in the lurch?
Well, no, not entirely.
It was partly that, sure –
 I saw the need and wanted to help,
 and I knew that if *I* didn't do something
 no one else would.
Yet there was more to it than that:
 pride for one thing –
 not wanting to be thought mean or selfish –

then the buzz that came from feeling useful,
valued,
indispensable,
the one who was always there when needed,
and finally there was cowardice –
a fear of looking someone in the eye and saying, without excuses,
'Not this time, no.'
There were a host of reasons, truth be told,
some easy to spot,
others hidden, even from me,
but deep down they amounted to this:
a sense that, as a person,
a friend
and a Christian,
declining wasn't an option;
that I had to say yes,
not because I wanted to,
but as a duty,
an obligation.
I was wrong,
deeply, dangerously wrong,
and I nearly paid the highest price.
I should have said no,
and I said yes,
again,
and again,
and again.
Don't make my mistake.
You can do your bit, like everyone else,
but you can't do it all,
and no one expects you to,
least of all God.

Further reading: 1 Corinthians 12:29-31

Are all apostles, all prophets, all teachers, all equipped with great powers? Do we all have the gift of healing, or tongues, or interpretation? But aim for the greater gifts, and I will show you an even better way.

Suggestions for action

If you've been meaning to take on a job or responsibility that you know you could and should be doing, volunteer now. If you're doing too much but haven't had the courage to say so, give something up even if there's no one else to take it on.

Closing prayer

Lord Jesus Christ,
    teach me when to say yes and when to say no,
    and help me not only to take those decisions
    but also to stick to them once taken.
Amen.

Sixth week

Luke: Ready to be there

Opening prayer

In darkness and in light,
  in trouble and in joy,
  help us to trust your love,
  to serve your purpose
  and to praise your name.
Through Jesus Christ our Lord.
Amen.

Daily Office Revised

Introduction

I put down the phone with a smile, heartened and encouraged. I hadn't solved anything it's true; nothing had changed, the situation no better than it had been before, except that I'd shared it with someone, been able to lighten the load, and, whatever else, I knew I was not alone. No, this isn't an advertisement for BT, though if they want to slip me a little commission I won't say no! It's an advertisement rather for Luke, yet another of the unsung heroes of the Bible. You see, we will all often have experiences like mine, or at least I hope we will; times when we share a problem, trouble or fear and gain strength from the very act of doing so. Not that it's only the bad things, of course; it's equally important to share our hopes and joys, triumphs and pleasures. To have someone there who cares is a priceless gift. Such a one was Luke. Few people in the New Testament can have had so little written about them yet have been so influential behind the scenes. He was not a preacher, as far as we know, nor one who in any way captured the headlines.

The one thing he is typically remembered for is being a doctor, and perhaps, through that, exercising a healing ministry. Yet Luke, I believe, was an exponent of one gift in a way few others could match, through his willingness simply to be there, a faithful friend in time of need. To me, that is not just a special *human* gift; it can also be a gift of the Spirit – one of the finest gifts of all.

Activity

Name the partner (see page 70).

Reading: 2 Timothy 4:9-11a

Do your best to come to me soon, for Demas, in love with this present world, has deserted me and gone to Thessalonica; Crescens has gone to Galatia, Titus to Dalmatia. Only Luke is with me. (*NRSV*)

Comment

Which important figure in the early Church travelled countless miles across numerous countries, working as a pioneer missionary to carry the gospel throughout a large part of the Roman world? The answer, of course, is the Apostle Paul, but that's not the only answer you could have given. You might equally have chosen Barnabas, who accompanied Paul in the first of his missionary journeys, or Silas, a faithful companion in the second. True, these names do not carry quite the same kudos as their illustrious colleague, but, as we have seen already with Barnabas, this does not mean that their contribution was negligible.

There's a third name, however, that might spring to mind still less readily, and that is the name Luke. 'Hang on,' you may say, 'I've heard of Luke. We all have.' And you'd be right; his name is

61

one that trips off the tongue along with Matthew, Mark and John. But, unless you're a New Testament scholar, he's not one you will readily associate with the journeys of Paul. Why? Quite simply because he is scarcely mentioned, not once directly referred to in the book of Acts and just a handful of times in the letters of Paul. Not much of a tribute. Still less to suggest he was a key figure in the Apostle's ministry or in the formative years of the Christian faith. Or is it? Paradoxically, it is this paucity of references that speaks most eloquently of Luke's character, reminding us that here was someone who made his contribution to the life of the Church behind the scenes, happy to be out of the limelight, hidden away in the background, unacknowledged and unrecognised. Little wonder, then, that the earliest manuscripts of his Gospel and its sequel, the book of Acts, have no name attached to them, and it has been left to tradition to record Luke as their author. Little wonder, also, that he does not mention himself by name in the saga of Acts, his natural humility keeping him firmly in the shadows.

There is one place in Scripture, however, that gives away both the nature of Luke's gift and just how much it meant to those around him, and we find it in our reading above, in the words, 'Only Luke is with me' (2 Timothy 4:11). It is the briefest of comments, but it is redolent with pathos and gratitude. For Paul, the end of his ministry was drawing near. He wrote, languishing in prison, thoughts turning to his old friends and companions, and as he remembers, so he rejoices that one at least is still with him, his loyal colleague Luke. Indeed, it may be that Luke was the one who penned these words at Paul's dictation, Paul frequently turning to another to act as scribe and secretary. Was Luke actually there, imprisoned with Paul? He could well have been, perhaps voluntarily choosing to share his incarceration. Or was he simply there in Rome, staying close by so as to bring in food and provisions, letters and greetings? Whatever the case, the fact that counted is that he *was* there, just as he had been with Paul so faithfully in the years leading up to that moment.

Precisely when or where the two first met is not clear, but a little detective work in reading the book of Acts reveals that Luke actively became involved in Paul's work at the start of his second missionary journey. The clue is in the sudden switch from 'they' to 'we', first found in Acts 16:10, and subsequently in 20:5 and 27:1. Suddenly, Luke is no longer simply relating what others have told him; he is writing first-hand of the events he was part of, the experiences he shared. When Paul set off to preach the gospel across Europe, Luke was there alongside him, travelling with him from Troas to Philippi. When Paul made his fateful journey to Jerusalem in the course of his third missionary expedition – a journey that was to lead to his arrest and subsequent imprisonment in Rome – once more, Luke was there. When Paul spent two years in custody in Caesarea, Luke was there yet again, as he was also in the shipwreck that followed on the way to Rome and in Paul's subsequent house-arrest, until, presumably, the end finally came. In other words, Luke was there through thick and thin; there when the going got tough, when the stakes were high and when the cost was clear.

There aren't many like Luke, are there? – people we can depend on when we're down on our luck and life goes pear-shaped. There aren't many who will happily share the bad times as well as the good, ready to share our privations and to sacrifice their time and money on our behalf. I doubt there are many either who would willingly devote themselves year in, year out to a particular cause without receiving some kind of public recognition and acknowledgement. That, though, is what we see in Luke – someone who was happy just to be there when needed. Never underestimate that gift, for it is one of the most precious there is, and one that each of us can show in our turn. It may not seem much – simply being there – yet it can mean more than words can begin to say. To be a listening ear, a helping hand, a shoulder to cry on, a sounding board for new ideas, is to offer a ministry that few can equal. It is to make Christ real, to embody him in the flesh, to be channels of his grace.

There will always be those like Paul called to be leaders, catching the eye with their story of faith and their public witness, but there will always also be far more whose journey is less dramatic and whose gifts are less on show. If you continue with that letter to

Timothy with which we started, or indeed with any of Paul's letters, you will find numerous other names, many mentioned just once in the Bible, yet clearly each shared and worked with Paul, perhaps even accompanying him on one of his journeys. The part they played goes unrecorded, but is no less real for that. Every one of them, in their own way, had exercised the gift of being there. In their silent witness, as in Luke's quiet but faithful ministry, lies a powerful reminder of the part *we* can play in the work of God's Spirit and the cause of his kingdom.

Summary

- Mention the missionary work of the early Church and our thoughts automatically turn to Paul. It is those who spearhead a project, leading from the front, who tend to be remembered.

- Luke scarcely receives a mention in the Bible, yet he was one of the most faithful companions of Paul, exercising his own very real ministry alongside that of his more celebrated colleague.

- Following his arrest in Jerusalem, Luke stayed with Paul to the end of his ministry, and presumably his life, while other friends and colleagues appear to have deserted him. Some were otherwise involved in the work of the Church, while Demas, it seems, had deserted his faith, 'in love with the present world' (2 Timothy 4:10).

- We do not know precisely what Luke did for Paul, or whether he shared his imprisonment, but we do know that he was there for him, and that his presence offered comfort, encouragement and inspiration.

- Our gift may not be in any way sensational, or even identified by most as a spiritual gift, but the act of being there for someone, to bear their burdens and share their joys and sorrows, is a ministry we should never underestimate.

- Most of us will exercise our gifts behind the scenes, often

1) What was Luke's special Ministry?

perhaps unrecognised. Sometimes, such 'hidden' gifts are the most valuable gifts of all.

What is the lesson of Luke's life? What do we learn of practical value for ourselves

Discussion *Peter & Sheila (divorce)*

- Are there times when someone has helped us simply through being there? What did their presence mean to us, and in what way was it needed? *Examples?*
- What things prevent us from being there for others as often as we should?
- What things stop us from telling those who are there for us just how much we value them?

Prayer

Loving God,
    we thank you for always being with us,
    whatever we may face,
    to strengthen, encourage, comfort and protect.
We thank you for those we can count on
    to be there when we need them,
    sharing our troubles and bearing our burdens,
    reassuring us that we are not alone.
Teach us to share that ministry in turn,
    ready to draw alongside those in any kind of need
    and to offer support and companionship.
Help us to understand
    that it is not so much the things we say
    or do that matter at such times,
    so much as being there.
So may we give expression to your love
    and embody your presence,
    to the glory of your name.
Amen.

Meditation of Luke

They think me special, some people,
    just because I wrote a Gospel.
Oh, it was an achievement of sorts, I grant you,
    and I'm glad I wrote it,
    for I had something to say and it needed saying,
    but it was about Jesus –
    what *he* achieved –
    not me.
I'm proud of one thing, though, I must admit,
    and that's learning today how much I meant to Paul.
I never realised, you see,
    never had any idea how important my contribution had been.
In fact, apart from my medical skills,
    I often doubted my usefulness completely,
    for I was very much one of the backroom boys,
    the supporting cast.
Paul was the one up front,
    taking the plaudits . . .
    and the flak . . .
    and alongside him were those like Barnabas, Silas, Timothy,
    each of them key personnel,
    respected figures,
    if not quite celebrities.
Me? I was just a scribe,
    there, if you like, to keep the minutes,
    record proceedings;
    and on occasions I felt insignificant,
    incidental,
    even perhaps superfluous to requirements.
But today, as he sat dictating a letter to Timothy,
    his voice quavered for a moment,
    breaking on the words, 'Only Luke is with me',
    and then he turned,
    his eyes meeting mine,

and on his face a smile of such gratitude,
such warmth –
a smile that said, 'Thank you, my friend.
Thank you for being there.'
It may not sound much,
but to me it was everything,
for suddenly I knew that simply through standing with him,
through sticking close,
I'd shared in his ministry,
and, through that, in the work of Christ.
I wrote a Gospel, it's true,
and yes, that's something to be proud of in a way,
but more important to me, I *lived* a gospel,
putting it simply into practice through faithful friendship
and quiet service;
so if you want to remember me,
if you really must,
then remember me for that.

Further reading: Galatians 6:2

Bear one another's burdens, and so fulfil the law of Christ. (*NRSV*)

Suggestions for action

Are there some you know of in need of a friend to stand alongside
them? Can you be that friend? If so, make time to write, call or visit,
not forcing yourself upon them but being there if wanted.

Closing prayer

Lord Jesus Christ,
as you have been there for me,
help me to be there for others,
for your name's sake.
Amen.

Appendix 1

Activities

First week: Ananias

Yes or no?

Select three volunteers from the group. Tell each one that they will be subjected in turn to a barrage of questions from the remaining group members to which they must only reply 'no'. The aim of the group is to make them say 'yes'. Afterwards, briefly consider those things they found it hardest and easiest to say no to, and then compare this to real-life situations we may face.

Second week: Barnabas

Lego® puzzle

The aim of this exercise is to simulate, as far as possible, the impact of encouragement and discouragement. You will need the disassembled pieces of a Lego® model, which you will either have to buy or borrow. Ask for a volunteer to be your 'builder', and briefly show him or her a picture of what you want him/her to make (specify a maximum time period of three minutes). Give the picture and instructions to the rest of the group, and instruct them in every way possible to discourage the person attempting to build the model. After three minutes, call a halt, assess the builder's efforts, and then disassemble the pieces once again. Ask your volunteer to have another go, and instruct the rest of the group this time to offer as much support and encouragement as possible. After a further three minutes, compare the success of this attempt with the last. Then, briefly discuss ways in which we can encourage and discourage, and consider the effect each of these may have.

Third week: James

Listen carefully

Prior to the session, record a variety of commonplace and not so commonplace sounds (for example, a dripping tap, a kettle boiling, a clock ticking). Ensure, if possible, that some are not immediately identifiable. Play the sounds to the group, giving time for them to identify each one before moving on to the next. Afterwards, discuss the importance of listening, exploring in particular the need to think and concentrate sometimes if we are to understand what it is we are hearing. Briefly discuss instances when we hear people without really listening to what they are saying.

Fourth week: Epaphras

Arm wrestling

Invite members of the group to take part in a light-hearted arm-wrestling competition. (Do not pressurise anyone who is unwilling or unable to take part.) Discuss afterwards the qualities needed for success, and briefly explore how we might relate this to prayer, considering in what others ways we might wrestle with something.

Fifth week: Epaphroditus

One load too many?

For this exercise, you will need the game Buckaroo®, or similar. The aim is simply to keep loading as much on to the model donkey as possible until a spring is triggered, causing it to fling off its load. If you have a large group, you may need to conduct two separate games, or two simultaneously, to give everyone a fair chance. Afterwards, briefly discuss the dangers of taking on too heavy a workload or other commitments, and ask if there have been occasions when group members have made such a mistake.

Sixth week: Luke

Name the partner

Ask the group to identify the faithful partner of each of the following (to avoid one or two individuals hogging the exercise, you might like to divide the group into two teams, handing over questions for a bonus in the unlikely event of an incorrect answer):

Batman

The Lone Ranger

Sherlock Holmes

Inspector Morse

Bertie Wooster

Dick Dastardly

Randall

Fagin

Sir Edmund Hillary

Robinson Crusoe

Appendix 2

Answers

Sixth week: Luke

Robin (Batman)

Tonto (The Lone Ranger)

Watson (Sherlock Holmes)

Sergeant Lewis (Inspector Morse)

Jeeves (Bertie Wooster)

Muttley (Dick Dastardly)

Hopkirk deceased (Randall)

The Artful Dodger (Fagin)

Sherpa Tenzing (Sir Edmund Hillary)

Man Friday (Robinson Crusoe)

Also in this series:
Living with questions – exploring faith and doubt
Paul – the man and the mission
Something to share – communicating the good news
Prayer – the fundamental questions
Love – the key to it all
Discipleship – the journey of faith
Women of faith – what they teach us

Also by Nick Fawcett:
No ordinary man (books 1 and 2)
Resources for reflective worship on the person of Jesus

The unfolding story
Resources for reflective worship on the Old Testament

Grappling with God (books 1-4)
Old Testament studies for personal and small-group use

To put it another way
Resources for reflective worship on the Parables

Are you listening?
Honest prayers about life

Prayers for all seasons (books 1 and 2)
A comprehensive resource for public worship

Getting it across
One hundred talks for family worship

Decisions, decisions
A Lent study course

Promises, promises
An Advent study course

Daily prayer
A book of daily devotions

All the above titles are available from your local Christian bookshop or direct from Kevin Mayhew Ltd, telephone 01449 737978, fax: 01449 737834, email: sales@kevinmayhewltd.com

ALL IN VAIN

Edited by

Chiara Cervasio

First published in Great Britain in 2004 by
ANCHOR BOOKS
Remus House,
Coltsfoot Drive,
Peterborough, PE2 9JX
Telephone (01733) 898102

SB ISBN 1 84418 321 1

FOREWORD

Anchor Books is a small press, established in 1992, with the aim of promoting readable poetry to as wide an audience as possible.

We hope to establish an outlet for writers of poetry who may have struggled to see their work in print.

The poems presented here have been selected from many entries, and as always editing proved to be a difficult task.

I trust this selection will delight and please the authors and all those who enjoy reading poetry.

Chiara Cervasio
Editor